THE

SISTERHOOD

OF

healing hearts

TO JACKIE, CARLA, DANIELLE,
HELEN, AMY, ANNETTE, AND TAMMI,
the original Sisterhood of Healing Hearts.
To all mothers trying to make it through every day while missing their child.

The Sisterhood of Healing Hearts Journal: Permission to Thrive. A Six Month Guided Journal for Grieving Mothers

Published by Kat Biggie Press
ISBN: 978-1-955119-54-2

Cover Design: Fresh Design
Formatting & interiro design by Margaret Cogswell

dear grieving MOTHER,

HOW DO YOU POSSIBLY HEAL A HEART THAT'S BEEN BROKEN BY THE LOSS OF A CHILD?

It seems like an impossible task.

One that may never be fully accomplished.

And it's true. Your heart will likely never fully heal.

However, it is possible to find joy and happiness again. It requires a concerted effort. It requires a choice on your part that this is what you want to do and a willingness to do the work. It also requires extending a lot of grace toward yourself and others.

If you're reading this, it means that you are ready and willing to take the steps to move through or continue your healing process after the loss of a pregnancy, infant, or child. You are making a conscious effort to choose joy rather than sadness. Or you are at least willing to try to get on that path.

Congratulations. This is a big step. It's one that others who have never experienced this type of loss will never fully understand, so I want to honor just how significant it is. Know and understand that this is a process that happens over time. Healing happens on your timeline, not on anyone else's. There may be setbacks and hard days, but the most important step is the one you take to heal today.

This guided journal incorporates activities to help you center and ground yourself, reconnect to yourself and encourage you to make time for self-care and self-love. We often overlook the importance of caring for ourselves when we are grieving. It's hard enough to make it through each day, but then add on the responsibilities of caring for other children or a spouse or partner, or working a busy job, and who has the time and energy to focus on caring for themselves? And yet, if you want to heal, you're going to have to put yourself first, even if only for a few minutes each day. The daily breathwork and gratitude exercises will calm you and help you heal your nervous system. Small activities like going for a walk or getting out in nature can completely change your disposition and reduce anxiety.

Let's address a common fear about healing after the loss of a pregnancy, infant, or child: If you're scared to heal, you're not alone. In the conversations I've had over the years with grieving mothers, I've encountered many mothers who feared healing, concerned that if they *healed* they will have forgotten their child. Or worse, they felt that it somehow made them a bad mother for moving forward in their lives. Let me reassure you that, even as healed as I may be now, there will forever be a Kathryn-shaped hole in my heart. I think about her daily, and I will always wonder how my life would be different today if she were still here.

Trust me, you will never forget. You will never be fully "over it." But that doesn't mean we have to stay in a place of pain and sadness. It doesn't mean we can't find peace.

I remember a time when I thought I'd never feel genuine happiness again. However, as I write this introduction, we are remembering the twelfth anniversary of my daughter's passing, and I can honestly say I am happy again. I consider myself as healed as a mother can be after the death of a child, even though I know I will never be the same person I was before her. I have not forgotten her in the healing process, and I will never forget her, but I am no longer actively grieving either.

Healing is not a straightforward journey. I am still faced with peaks and valleys. Sometimes I still experience an overwhelming sense of sadness, especially around significant dates and milestones. But to heal, one must make the choice to acknowledge the pain, sadness, anger, disappointment, guilt, and all the other emotions we experience after the loss of a child, work through them, and try our best to pick ourselves up and move forward even when that seems impossible.

There will be many days that this is a challenge. I encourage you to find the people in your life who care about you the most and pull them in closely.

Don't be surprised if these are not the same people you were close with before your child died. You will likely make new friends with whom you will form strong bonds after your loss.

Community has been a tremendous part of my healing. In the months after my daughter died, I found Facebook groups with other mothers who walked a similar path. I found other people who knew and understood the pain of significant loss. And they provided an outlet for me that most people in my life were unable to. The grieving mother community has been a tremendous source of strength for me because they truly understand what I have been through, validate my feelings, and share similar stories.

Whoever your inner circle is, find those people and make time to connect. Your best friend, siblings, neighbor, new friends, whomever they may be. Your spouse, who is grieving too. Don't forget to lean on each other.

A Harvard Study of Adult Development, which spanned seventy-five years, examined what makes people the happiest. The results were clear. The answer is in community and deep relationships. Close-knit relationships provide shelter against loneliness and sadness.

Losing a child is a significantly isolating event. It might be easiest for you to turn away from the people who love you the most, but I encourage you to let them in. Or if you can't, find a new community that understands you. In this journal, in the quarterly check-ins, you'll find space to write about existing and new relationships. You might be angry or disappointed with the people you love the most. You might find new people who bring you joy.

Take the time to reflect on the changes you see in yourself and others.

HOW DO YOU KNOW WHAT WILL HELP ME HEAL?

I'm not a therapist, a guru, or a spiritual healer in any capacity. I'm just a mother who lost a child and like you, had to figure out my way through the muck to get back to living life again. This journal is the culmination of what I believe are the things that were the most helpful to me. I remember all too well how overwhelming the first few months/years can be; how difficult it can be to concentrate, to get anything done at all. I've designed this journal in a way that I hope will encourage you to do activities that can help you heal, while not being too overwhelming or requiring too much effort on your part to do them. Meet yourself where you're at. Do what you can do, even if it's a very small effort in the beginning and challenge yourself to get stronger and do more as time passes and you feel able to do so.

The truth is, I don't know what will help YOU specifically. But I do know there is a lot of research-based evidence on the four key components in this journal and how they can help a person heal: breathwork, gratitude practices & writing, making time for self-care, and focusing on relationships and community.

People often ask me what I did to heal.

The answer is: in the beginning, I did what I had to do every day to survive that day. Trust me when I say, if there's a coping mechanism, I've tried it. Not all of my coping methods were healthy: retail therapy, self-numbing, overeating, isolating myself, keeping myself so busy I had no time to grieve, avoiding my real feelings.

Over time, life began to get a little easier, and I made a choice that I did not want to fall into an abyss of sadness. So I began incorporating healthier choices. I found a grief support network. I tried therapy, yoga, spiritual journeys, complete health revolutions, running and attending retreats, meditations, exercise, and more. I turned to writing and journaling and found this to be especially helpful in processing my grief. It is also helpful when I help others through my blogging and books.

I became certified as a Grief Recovery specialist, joined a program to become certified in Emotional Freedom Technique (EFT) Tapping, and made it halfway through a yoga certification program. These training programs taught me the importance of breathwork and other activities to calm the nervous system. They reinforced the importance of making time to calm your brain, which for me came largely through writing and journaling, tapping, making time to breathe, and choosing self-care activities.

I read books and sought out podcasts on healing and learned that some of the happiest people are those who serve others and practice daily gratitude. So I incorporated those activities into my personal life.

These are some of the activities that made the biggest difference for me:

- Making the choice to change my thoughts and feelings by focusing on joy
- Grounding myself through going for walks, getting out in nature, and hugging trees (yes, it's a real thing and trees have amazing energy!).
- Laughing as often as possible.
- Spending time doing things that make me feel better. Water is one of those outlets, and I go to the water as often as I can. Nature is good!
- Surrounding myself with people who lifted me up and make me feel seen and heard.
- Crying and grieving when I need to do so.
- Making the time to breathe deeply.
- Practicing gratitude.
- Serving others through blogging, writing books, starting a nonprofit to provide care packages at no charge to support grieving mothers, running retreats, volunteering, finding ways to advocate for programs that help women and children, and etc.
- Finding ways to keep her memory alive every day.

I am living my life to honor her short one. I am present in this life. I make the conscious choice each day to move forward, to seek healing, to find joy.

It is my wish for you that you will find healing, joy, and happiness as well. It starts with you making the choice that you want to heal.

how to use this JOURNAL

The activities in this journal are designed to guide you through daily, weekly, monthly, and quarterly healing activities in the most gentle way possible. If you're ever overwhelmed with the activities, step away. The daily and weekly activities have a suggested timeline, but I encourage you to make it fit in YOUR timeline.

1. Give yourself time each day if possible to at least open the journal and look at the activities. I know in the beginning, it can be so challenging to even get out of bed, let alone make time for ourselves, or to remember additional tasks, like breathwork and gratitude.
2. Pick the time of day you're most likely to be successful in journaling. Maybe set the journal with your coffee cup, or someplace to easily remind you in your morning routine. Or set it by your bedside table to look at before you go to sleep.
3. Get some fun, sparkly pens. You might want to doodle or draw in the journal, not just write. I find fun colors lift me up.
4. Give yourself grace. This journal is not dated. You can start at any time. You can take time off. Do this on your own timeline. You may need to take a break and come back to it later. It contains six months of activities, but if it takes you twelve months, that is perfectly okay. The most important part is that you're taking action steps to heal!

The activities focus on the following core elements:

- Breathwork
- Gratitude
- Self-care
- Journaling

BREATHWORK

You're encouraged to find a moment each day to breathe deeply. Most of us do not breathe in deeply enough, resulting in the brain having less oxygen. This makes us tired, foggy, and feel worse. Even a few minutes of deep breathing can make a significant difference in your day. Once you've done some deep breaths, color in the heart that indicates you've completed this daily practice.

GRATITUDE

It can be difficult to practice gratitude when we've suffered such an enormous loss and are angry at the entire world. Even if you can only find one thing a week to be grateful for—even if that one thing is just, "I am grateful I am Kathryn's mother"—try to find something you can be grateful for. Write it down. If you're really struggling, pick one of the affirmations you like and write that.

SELF-CARE

Self-care covers a wide range of activities and is dependent on what you enjoy doing. Self-care activities do not have to cost any money or be difficult to plan. The purpose of self-care is to focus on YOU. Make time for YOU. Making time to journal and heal is in of itself a huge act of self-care and self-love. A very simple act of self-care you can do daily is to walk or spend some time outdoors or in nature. I've found walking to be one of the greatest cures of anxiety and calms me.

During my heaviest times of grief, which was certainly partly due to the fact that I had three small children I also had to care for, self-care fell to the wayside. I had a very creative friend, Tova "Muchness" Gould, who started the Muchness Movement. She'd also lost her identical twin daughters to Twin-to-Twin Transfusion Syndrome, and in her healing, she decided that bright, fun, sparkly objects were what she needed to feel better. Through her "muchness" movement, Tova encourages women to find the things in life that made them feel sparkly and happy.

I'd never been a very girly girl, and no one would describe me as "sparkly," so I was just as surprised as everyone else when during my healing time, I found joy in glittery headbands and bright nail polishes.

You never know where your inspiration is going to come from or what is going to make you feel better. But digging into your own "muchness" might make you smile. Through this, I found myself seeking other ways to take care of myself. I started wearing bright colors. Eventually I got a beautiful butterfly tattooed on my back. I dyed my hair purple (that was a lot of muchness!) to support the March of Dimes and threw myself into fundraising for this organization to support their research and efforts to support healthy pregnancies and babies.

Try new things for self-care. The goal is make yourself feel better. It may come in surprising ways. I've provided a self-care ideas bank below that can help you identify some things to do in the beginning when it may be hard. If you're able to, you might get a little extravagant. But even simple actions of self-love can provide much needed healing.

JOURNALING

I cannot begin to express how much healing has come from writing for me. This may not be your outlet, but there is a lot of research behind the power of writing. Whether in a journal, blog, notebook, or scrap of paper, writing can often help you release what is trapped within, and I almost always feel better after journaling about my thoughts and feelings. You can do this in many ways. I've provided prompts and space throughout this journal to write.

If you're afraid of anyone finding what you've written, rip the page out and burn it. That also feels great! If writing is too overwhelming, take a step back from it.

I have also included some space for you to write about upcoming events and milestones. Write it all down. You can help prevent sad days by looking forward and identifying what is coming up that may be challenging for you to handle. You might write about the following things: What are the things that are likely to trigger you this week or month? What's going to be difficult this week? How can you ask for help? Who can you ask for help? How can you think about it differently? What coping skills can you use?

Of course, you don't have to follow the prompts. Write whatever you want. Just write. One day, you may want to come back and reread what you've written so you can see how far you've come and how much you've grown. Or you might choose to burn the whole thing and move on. That's up to you!

CHECK-INS

You'll have monthly and quarterly check-ins as well. These are designed to help you reflect on the healing that has happened as well as what is coming up. The quarterly check-ins have a heavy emphasis on your relationships.

Between each month and throughout the journal, you'll find affirmations. Stating affirmations daily or on some regular basis can help you minimize negativity and replace bad thoughts with positive thoughts. The affirmations may not all resonate with you. But find the ones that do, and repeat them as often as you want. You deserve to be happy, mama, and sometimes we have to retrain our brains to believe that!

begin your healing when you're READY AND ON YOUR TERMS

Probably the most important lesson I have learned in the past twelve years is that no one's grief journey is the same as another's. We may share similar feelings and experiences, but some of us heal quickly while it may take years for others to find a place of peace. Understand and know you will have setbacks. But pick yourself up and keep trying.

I believe the ultimate path to healing is to Choose Joy. I choose joy. Every day I make the choice to take care of myself and to love myself. Some days I'm more successful than others. But I'm still moving forward. And please remember, sometimes choosing joy is not enough. Don't be afraid to seek out professional help.

You are not alone in this journey. And you are so very loved.

With deepest gratitude for you,

Alexa

Alexa Haddock Bigwarfe

Mother to Braedan, Ella, Charis, and our sweet angel, Kathryn

Additional resources: For book and podcast suggestions, as well as additional resources to help you in your grieving process, please visit https://sunshineafterthestorm.org/resources

SELF-CARE IDEAS BANK

This bank is designed to help you if you're in a slump, have never taken time for self-care before, or just need some inspiration. The list is certainly not all-encompassing. You're encouraged to try any activity that you feel takes care of YOU and makes YOU feel better.

- Go for a walk
- Get out into nature
- Hug a tree
- Call a friend
- Watch a funny movie
- Take a hot bath with Epsom salts
- Get a facial
- Get a massage
- Go on a girls' weekend
- Try a float tank
- Find a meditation you enjoy and listen to it
- Try a yoga class
- Get certified as a yoga instructor
- Paint your nails a fun color
- Dye your hair
- Cut your hair
- Get some new clothes
- Volunteer someplace
- Send a grieving mother a care package
- Start a blog
- Read a book
- Write a book
- Say your affirmations daily
- Plant a tree in honor of your child
- Make a donation in honor of your child
- Plan a trip (and go on it!)
- Go for a hike
- Get a tattoo
- Cry
- Laugh
- Go out for dinner
- Order in a meal
- Do a craft
- Color something
- Write a short story
- Have a bonfire
- Drink a glass of wine
- Take an art class
- Paint something
- Go running
- Run a 5K
- Join a gym
- Exercise daily
- Listen to encouraging podcasts
- Turn up the radio on fun, energizing songs
- Make a collage of your favorite pictures
- Start a garden
- Buy yourself flowers
- Go shopping
- Change up your decorations in your house
- Bake something - and enjoy eating it!
- Hug yourself
- Have a date night
- Plant and nurture a garden
- Write in your journal
- Drink more water!
- Go sit by a waterfall or river or lake
- Go to a concert
- Go to a fundraiser for an important cause
- Start a fundraiser for an important cause
- Eat some chocolate
- Try something new!

What sounds fun to you?

AFFIRMATION IDEAS BANK

- You are with me even when I can't see you.
- I am taking steps, however small, towards healing.
- It's okay to find joy without feeling guilt.
- My emotional strength is building, day by day.
- I give myself permission to live fully, even while I grieve.
- Each day I heal a little more, and I acknowledge that progress.
- I am worthy of happiness and love, now and always.
- I trust the journey of my heart's healing.
- It's okay to prioritize my own well-being.
- My happiness is its own form of honoring you.
- Healing is not a betrayal of your memory; it's a tribute to our love.
- I embrace the support and love of others as I heal.
- Every step forward is a victory worth celebrating.
- It's okay to let go of pain while keeping the love intact.
- I am resilient, and my resilience honors you.
- I am actively seeking peace and emotional balance in my life.
- I honor my own life by embracing joy whenever I can.
- My well-being is a testament to the strength of my spirit.
- My growth and happiness can coexist with my grief.
- It's okay to seek professional help to guide my healing journey.
- I am not alone in my healing; I am supported and loved.
- I am reclaiming my zest for life, one moment at a time.
- I am deserving of self-care and self-love.
- I allow myself to feel, process, and then let go.
- My capacity for joy is expanding, even as I remember you.
- I am learning to navigate a world that is different but beautiful.

I AM TAKING STEPS,
however small,
TOWARDS HEALING.

month 1 ______________________________

SUN	MON	TUE	WED	THU	FRI	SAT

week of ____________ to ____________

remember your BREATHWORK

Set a timer for 2 minutes each day just to breathe deeply. Breathe in deeply through your nose for a count of 4-6 and then slowly release that breath. If you can't do two full minutes, start by trying to breathe deeply in and out at least 3 times until you can increase the time. Conscious breath-work reduces the effects of PTSD and stress from trauma. It promotes calmness and well-being.

Check off or color in the heart for each day you successfully did your breathwork and then write how you felt after your breath-work session.

M ♡ ____________________

T ♡ ____________________

W ♡ ____________________

T ♡ ____________________

F ♡ ____________________

S ♡ ____________________

S ♡ ____________________

practice your GRATITUDE

Finish this sentence each day: TODAY I AM GRATEFUL FOR...
If you're struggling to find gratitude, choose from the Affirmation Bank in the front of the planner and write it in each day.

M

T

W

T

F

S

S

practice your SELF-CARE

Color in a heart for each self-care activity you did this week.

MAKING TIME FOR SELF-CARE

Try to fit in small moments of self-care when possible. What did you do this week? How did you feel? If it's too much to journal, simply color in a heart when you do something good for yourself.

how did you FEEL THIS WEEK?

Use the following pages to draw or write about your week. What things happened? Were there any triggering events? How did you handle them? Are you making time to care for yourself and how does that feel? Are you choosing joy? Looking forward to next week, is anything coming up that might be difficult to handle?

week of ____________ to ____________

remember your BREATHWORK

Set a timer for 2 minutes each day just to breathe deeply. Breathe in deeply through your nose for a count of 4-6 and then slowly release that breath. If you can't do two full minutes, start by trying to breathe deeply in and out at least 3 times until you can increase the time. Conscious breathwork reduces the effects of PTSD and stress from trauma. It promotes calmness and well-being.

Check off or color in the heart for each day you successfully did your breathwork and then write how you felt after your breathwork session.

M ♡ ______________________________

T ♡ ______________________________

W ♡ ______________________________

T ♡ ______________________________

F ♡ ______________________________

S ♡ ______________________________

S ♡ ______________________________

practice your GRATITUDE

Finish this sentence each day: TODAY I AM GRATEFUL FOR...
If you're struggling to find gratitude, choose from the Affirmation Bank in the front of the planner and write it in each day.

M ♡ ______________________________

____

____

T ♡ ______________________________

____

____

W ♡ ______________________________

____

____

T ♡ ______________________________

____

____

F ♡ ______________________________

____

____

S ♡ ______________________________

____

____

S ♡ ______________________________

____

____

Color in a heart for each self-care activity you did this week.

MAKING TIME FOR SELF-CARE

Try to fit in small moments of self-care when possible. What did you do this week? How did you feel? If it's too much to journal, simply color in a heart when you do something good for yourself.

how did you FEEL THIS WEEK?

Use the following pages to draw or write about your week. What things happened? Were there any triggering events? How did you handle them? Are you making time to care for yourself and how does that feel? Are you choosing joy? Looking forward to next week, is anything coming up that might be difficult to handle?

week of ____________ to ____________

remember your BREATHWORK

Set a timer for 2 minutes each day just to breathe deeply. Breathe in deeply through your nose for a count of 4-6 and then slowly release that breath. If you can't do two full minutes, start by trying to breathe deeply in and out at least 3 times until you can increase the time. Conscious breathwork reduces the effects of PTSD and stress from trauma. It promotes calmness and well-being.

Check off or color in the heart for each day you successfully did your breathwork and then write how you felt after your breathwork session.

M ♡ ____________________

T ♡ ____________________

W ♡ ____________________

T ♡ ____________________

F ♡ ____________________

S ♡ ____________________

S ♡ ____________________

practice your GRATITUDE

Finish this sentence each day: TODAY I AM GRATEFUL FOR...
If you're struggling to find gratitude, choose from the Affirmation Bank in the front of the planner and write it in each day.

M ♡ ______________________________

T ♡ ______________________________

W ♡ ______________________________

T ♡ ______________________________

F ♡ ______________________________

S ♡ ______________________________

S ♡ ______________________________

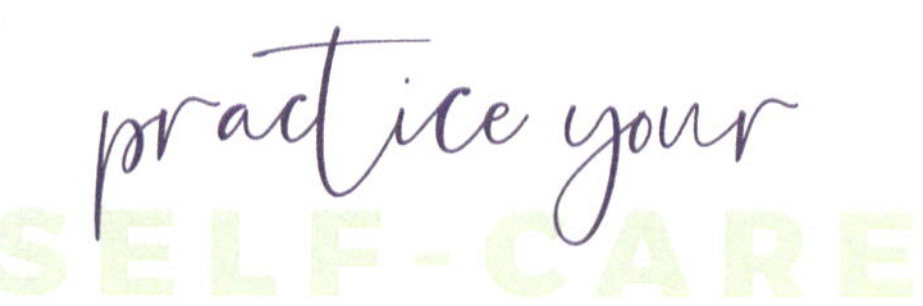

Color in a heart for each self-care activity you did this week.

MAKING TIME FOR SELF-CARE

Try to fit in small moments of self-care when possible. What did you do this week? How did you feel? If it's too much to journal, simply color in a heart when you do something good for yourself.

how did you FEEL THIS WEEK?

Use the following pages to draw or write about your week. What things happened? Were there any triggering events? How did you handle them? Are you making time to care for yourself and how does that feel? Are you choosing joy? Looking forward to next week, is anything coming up that might be difficult to handle?

week of ____________ to ____________

remember your BREATHWORK

Set a timer for 2 minutes each day just to breathe deeply. Breathe in deeply through your nose for a count of 4-6 and then slowly release that breath. If you can't do two full minutes, start by trying to breathe deeply in and out at least 3 times until you can increase the time. Conscious breathwork reduces the effects of PTSD and stress from trauma. It promotes calmness and well-being.

Check off or color in the heart for each day you successfully did your breathwork and then write how you felt after your breathwork session.

M ♡ ____________________

T ♡ ____________________

W ♡ ____________________

T ♡ ____________________

F ♡ ____________________

S ♡ ____________________

S ♡ ____________________

practice your GRATITUDE

Finish this sentence each day: TODAY I AM GRATEFUL FOR...
If you're struggling to find gratitude, choose from the Affirmation Bank in the front of the planner and write it in each day.

M ♡ ______________________________

T ♡ ______________________________

W ♡ ______________________________

T ♡ ______________________________

F ♡ ______________________________

S ♡ ______________________________

S ♡ ______________________________

Color in a heart for each self-care activity you did this week.

MAKING TIME FOR SELF-CARE

Try to fit in small moments of self-care when possible. What did you do this week? How did you feel? If it's too much to journal, simply color in a heart when you do something good for yourself.

how did you FEEL THIS WEEK?

Use the following pages to draw or write about your week. What things happened? Were there any triggering events? How did you handle them? Are you making time to care for yourself and how does that feel? Are you choosing joy? Looking forward to next week, is anything coming up that might be difficult to handle?

week of ____________ to ____________

remember your BREATHWORK

Set a timer for 2 minutes each day just to breathe deeply. Breathe in deeply through your nose for a count of 4-6 and then slowly release that breath. If you can't do two full minutes, start by trying to breathe deeply in and out at least 3 times until you can increase the time. Conscious breath-work reduces the effects of PTSD and stress from trauma. It promotes calmness and well-being.

Check off or color in the heart for each day you successfully did your breathwork and then write how you felt after your breath-work session.

M ♡ ____

T ♡ ____

W ♡ ____

T ♡ ____

F ♡ ____

S ♡ ____

S ♡ ____

practice your GRATITUDE

Finish this sentence each day: TODAY I AM GRATEFUL FOR...
If you're struggling to find gratitude, choose from the Affirmation Bank in the front of the planner and write it in each day.

M ♡ ____________________

T ♡ ____________________

W ♡ ____________________

T ♡ ____________________

F ♡ ____________________

S ♡ ____________________

S ♡ ____________________

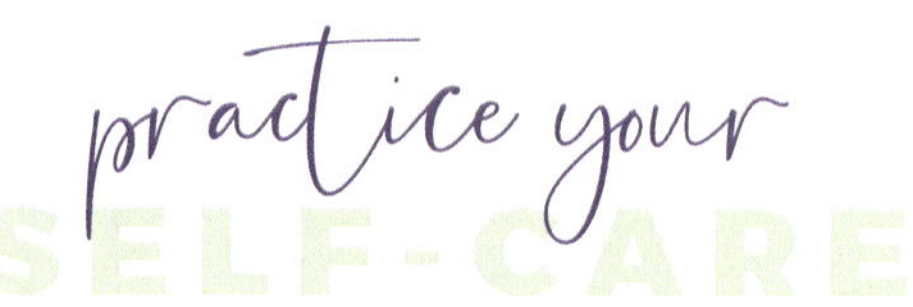

Color in a heart for each self-care activity you did this week.

MAKING TIME FOR SELF-CARE

Try to fit in small moments of self-care when possible. What did you do this week? How did you feel? If it's too much to journal, simply color in a heart when you do something good for yourself.

how did you FEEL THIS WEEK?

Use the following pages to draw or write about your week. What things happened? Were there any triggering events? How did you handle them? Are you making time to care for yourself and how does that feel? Are you choosing joy? Looking forward to next week, is anything coming up that might be difficult to handle?

REFLECTION

You've made it a month! Are you noticing any changes in how you feel? How are your emotions? Did you experience any aha moments? Are you making time for yourself? What about the important people in your life? Use these pages to write or draw your observations about the past month.

monthly CHECK-IN

SELF-CARE

Fill in a heart for each week you did at least 2 self-care activities.

♡ ♡ ♡ ♡ ♡

WHICH SELF-CARE ACTIVITIES DID YOU DO AND HOW DID YOU FEEL AFTER COMPLETING THEM?

THINGS TO TRY

List what you want to add to your self-care next month. Refer to the self-care ideas bank if you need inspiration.

monthly CHECK-IN

REACHING OUT

It's easy to get lost in our own pain and shut out the other important members of our lives. Remember: the people who are the happiest have strong relationships with others. While it may be difficult to reach out in a time that you feel people should be checking in on you, try not to isolate yourself.

Who are the important people in your life? Who will you make an effort to reach out to? If you have other children, how are they doing? How is your spouse? Who is someone you were close to before that you haven't heard from in a while?

List three people you commit to reaching out to via text, phone call, email, snail mail, or getting together with. Think about birthdays, anniversaries, and other special events and list those out. Be sure to add to your calendar.

I WILL REACH OUT TO...

♡ ______________________________

♡ ______________________________

♡ ______________________________

UPCOMING EVENTS INCLUDE...

____

____

____

____

____

____

IT'S OKAY TO

find joy

WITHOUT
FEELING GUILT.

month 2 ______________________

SUN	MON	TUE	WED	THU	FRI	SAT

week of ______________ to ______________

Set a timer for 2 minutes each day just to breathe deeply. Breathe in deeply through your nose for a count of 4-6 and then slowly release that breath. If you can't do two full minutes, start by trying to breathe deeply in and out at least 3 times until you can increase the time. Conscious breathwork reduces the effects of PTSD and stress from trauma. It promotes calmness and well-being.

Check off or color in the heart for each day you successfully did your breathwork and then write how you felt after your breathwork session.

M ♡ ______________________________

T ♡ ______________________________

W ♡ ______________________________

T ♡ ______________________________

F ♡ ______________________________

S ♡ ______________________________

S ♡ ______________________________

practice your GRATITUDE

Finish this sentence each day: TODAY I AM GRATEFUL FOR...
If you're struggling to find gratitude, choose from the Affirmation Bank in the front of the planner and write it in each day.

M ♡ ______

T ♡ ______

W ♡ ______

T ♡ ______

F ♡ ______

S ♡ ______

S ♡ ______

practice your SELF-CARE

Color in a heart for each self-care activity you did this week.

♡

____

____

♡

____

____

♡

____

____

♡

____

____

♡

____

____

MAKING TIME FOR SELF-CARE

Try to fit in small moments of self-care when possible. What did you do this week? How did you feel? If it's too much to journal, simply color in a heart when you do something good for yourself.

how did you FEEL THIS WEEK?

Use the following pages to draw or write about your week. What things happened? Were there any triggering events? How did you handle them? Are you making time to care for yourself and how does that feel? Are you choosing joy? Looking forward to next week, is anything coming up that might be difficult to handle?

week of ______________ to ______________

remember your BREATHWORK

Set a timer for 2 minutes each day just to breathe deeply. Breathe in deeply through your nose for a count of 4-6 and then slowly release that breath. If you can't do two full minutes, start by trying to breathe deeply in and out at least 3 times until you can increase the time. Conscious breathwork reduces the effects of PTSD and stress from trauma. It promotes calmness and well-being.

Check off or color in the heart for each day you successfully did your breathwork and then write how you felt after your breathwork session.

M ♡ ______________________________

T ♡ ______________________________

W ♡ ______________________________

T ♡ ______________________________

F ♡ ______________________________

S ♡ ______________________________

S ♡ ______________________________

practice your GRATITUDE

Finish this sentence each day: TODAY I AM GRATEFUL FOR...
If you're struggling to find gratitude, choose from the Affirmation Bank in the front of the planner and write it in each day.

M ♡ ____________________

T ♡ ____________________

W ♡ ____________________

T ♡ ____________________

F ♡ ____________________

S ♡ ____________________

S ♡ ____________________

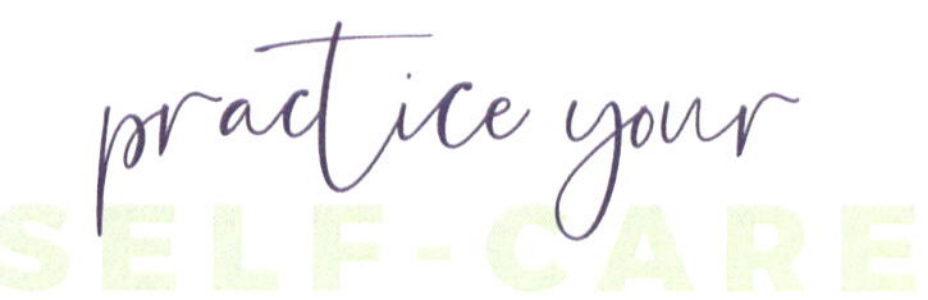

practice your SELF-CARE

Color in a heart for each self-care activity you did this week.

♡

____

____

♡

____

____

♡

____

____

♡

____

____

♡

____

____

MAKING TIME FOR SELF-CARE

Try to fit in small moments of self-care when possible. What did you do this week? How did you feel? If it's too much to journal, simply color in a heart when you do something good for yourself.

how did you FEEL THIS WEEK?

Use the following pages to draw or write about your week. What things happened? Were there any triggering events? How did you handle them? Are you making time to care for yourself and how does that feel? Are you choosing joy? Looking forward to next week, is anything coming up that might be difficult to handle?

week of ____________ to ____________

Set a timer for 2 minutes each day just to breathe deeply. Breathe in deeply through your nose for a count of 4-6 and then slowly release that breath. If you can't do two full minutes, start by trying to breathe deeply in and out at least 3 times until you can increase the time. Conscious breath-work reduces the effects of PTSD and stress from trauma. It promotes calmness and well-being.

Check off or color in the heart for each day you successfully did your breathwork and then write how you felt after your breath-work session.

M ♡ ____________________

T ♡ ____________________

W ♡ ____________________

T ♡ ____________________

F ♡ ____________________

S ♡ ____________________

S ♡ ____________________

practice your GRATITUDE

Finish this sentence each day: TODAY I AM GRATEFUL FOR...
If you're struggling to find gratitude, choose from the Affirmation Bank in the front of the planner and write it in each day.

M ♡ ______________________________

____

____

T ♡ ______________________________

____

____

W ♡ ______________________________

____

____

T ♡ ______________________________

____

____

F ♡ ______________________________

____

____

S ♡ ______________________________

____

____

S ♡ ______________________________

____

____

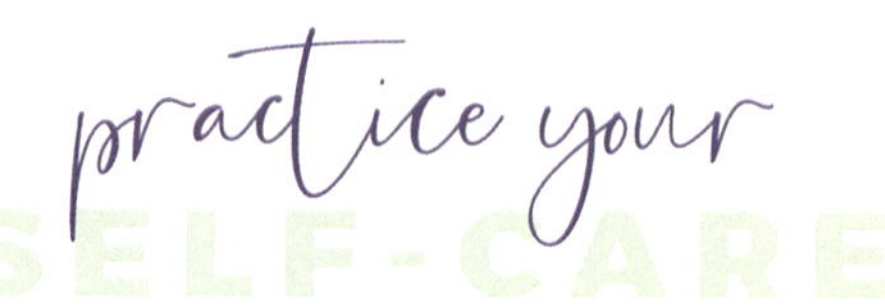

Color in a heart for each self-care activity you did this week.

♡

♡

♡

♡

♡

MAKING TIME FOR SELF-CARE

Try to fit in small moments of self-care when possible. What did you do this week? How did you feel? If it's too much to journal, simply color in a heart when you do something good for yourself.

how did you FEEL THIS WEEK?

Use the following pages to draw or write about your week. What things happened? Were there any triggering events? How did you handle them? Are you making time to care for yourself and how does that feel? Are you choosing joy? Looking forward to next week, is anything coming up that might be difficult to handle?

week of ______________ to ______________

Set a timer for 2 minutes each day just to breathe deeply. Breathe in deeply through your nose for a count of 4-6 and then slowly release that breath. If you can't do two full minutes, start by trying to breathe deeply in and out at least 3 times until you can increase the time. Conscious breathwork reduces the effects of PTSD and stress from trauma. It promotes calmness and well-being.

Check off or color in the heart for each day you successfully did your breathwork and then write how you felt after your breathwork session.

M ♡ ______________________________

T ♡ ______________________________

W ♡ ______________________________

T ♡ ______________________________

F ♡ ______________________________

S ♡ ______________________________

S ♡ ______________________________

practice your GRATITUDE

Finish this sentence each day: TODAY I AM GRATEFUL FOR...
If you're struggling to find gratitude, choose from the Affirmation Bank in the front of the planner and write it in each day.

M ♡ ______________________________

T ♡ ______________________________

W ♡ ______________________________

T ♡ ______________________________

F ♡ ______________________________

S ♡ ______________________________

S ♡ ______________________________

Color in a heart for each self-care activity you did this week.

MAKING TIME FOR SELF-CARE

Try to fit in small moments of self-care when possible. What did you do this week? How did you feel? If it's too much to journal, simply color in a heart when you do something good for yourself.

how did you FEEL THIS WEEK?

Use the following pages to draw or write about your week. What things happened? Were there any triggering events? How did you handle them? Are you making time to care for yourself and how does that feel? Are you choosing joy? Looking forward to next week, is anything coming up that might be difficult to handle?

week of ____________ to ____________

remember your BREATHWORK

Set a timer for 2 minutes each day just to breathe deeply. Breathe in deeply through your nose for a count of 4-6 and then slowly release that breath. If you can't do two full minutes, start by trying to breathe deeply in and out at least 3 times until you can increase the time. Conscious breath-work reduces the effects of PTSD and stress from trauma. It promotes calmness and well-being.

Check off or color in the heart for each day you successfully did your breathwork and then write how you felt after your breath-work session.

M ♡ ____________________

T ♡ ____________________

W ♡ ____________________

T ♡ ____________________

F ♡ ____________________

S ♡ ____________________

S ♡ ____________________

practice your GRATITUDE

Finish this sentence each day: TODAY I AM GRATEFUL FOR...

If you're struggling to find gratitude, choose from the Affirmation Bank in the front of the planner and write it in each day.

M ♡ ______

T ♡ ______

W ♡ ______

T ♡ ______

F ♡ ______

S ♡ ______

S ♡ ______

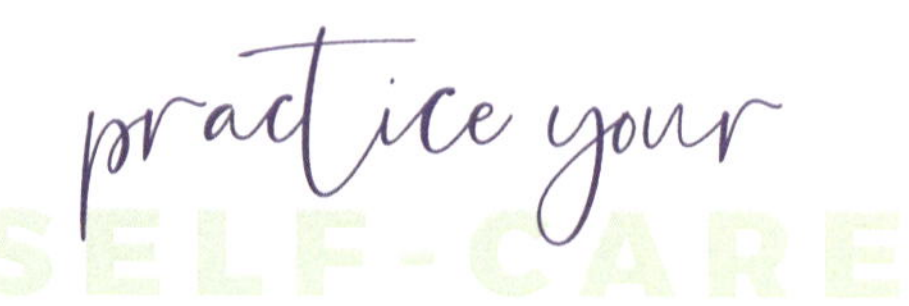

Color in a heart for each self-care activity you did this week.

MAKING TIME FOR SELF-CARE

Try to fit in small moments of self-care when possible. What did you do this week? How did you feel? If it's too much to journal, simply color in a heart when you do something good for yourself.

how did you FEEL THIS WEEK?

Use the following pages to draw or write about your week. What things happened? Were there any triggering events? How did you handle them? Are you making time to care for yourself and how does that feel? Are you choosing joy? Looking forward to next week, is anything coming up that might be difficult to handle?

REFLECTION

You've made it a month! Are you noticing any changes in how you feel? How are your emotions? Did you experience any aha moments? Are you making time for yourself? What about the important people in your life? Use these pages to write or draw your observations about the past month.

monthly CHECK-IN

SELF-CARE

Fill in a heart for each week you did at least 2 self-care activities.

♡ ♡ ♡ ♡ ♡

WHICH SELF-CARE ACTIVITIES DID YOU DO AND HOW DID YOU FEEL AFTER COMPLETING THEM?

THINGS TO TRY

List what you want to add to your self-care next month. Refer to the self-care ideas bank if you need inspiration.

monthly CHECK-IN

REACHING OUT

It's easy to get lost in our own pain and shut out the other important members of our lives. Remember: the people who are the happiest have strong relationships with others. While it may be difficult to reach out in a time that you feel people should be checking in on you, try not to isolate yourself.

Who are the important people in your life? Who will you make an effort to reach out to? If you have other children, how are they doing? How is your spouse? Who is someone you were close to before that you haven't heard from in a while?

List three people you commit to reaching out to via text, phone call, email, snail mail, or getting together with. Think about birthdays, anniversaries, and other special events and list those out. Be sure to add to your calendar.

I WILL REACH OUT TO...

♡ ____________________

♡ ____________________

♡ ____________________

UPCOMING EVENTS INCLUDE...

____

____

____

____

____

____

MY EMOTIONAL

strength

IS BUILDING
DAY BY DAY.

month 3 ____________________

SUN	MON	TUE	WED	THU	FRI	SAT

week of ____________ to ____________

remember your BREATHWORK

Set a timer for 2 minutes each day just to breathe deeply. Breathe in deeply through your nose for a count of 4-6 and then slowly release that breath. If you can't do two full minutes, start by trying to breathe deeply in and out at least 3 times until you can increase the time. Conscious breathwork reduces the effects of PTSD and stress from trauma. It promotes calmness and well-being.

Check off or color in the heart for each day you successfully did your breathwork and then write how you felt after your breathwork session.

M ♡ ____________________

T ♡ ____________________

W ♡ ____________________

T ♡ ____________________

F ♡ ____________________

S ♡ ____________________

S ♡ ____________________

practice your GRATITUDE

Finish this sentence each day: TODAY I AM GRATEFUL FOR...
If you're struggling to find gratitude, choose from the Affirmation Bank in the front of the planner and write it in each day.

M ♡ ______________________________

____

____

T ♡ ______________________________

____

____

W ♡ ______________________________

____

____

T ♡ ______________________________

____

____

F ♡ ______________________________

____

____

S ♡ ______________________________

____

____

S ♡ ______________________________

____

____

Color in a heart for each self-care activity you did this week.

MAKING TIME FOR SELF-CARE

Try to fit in small moments of self-care when possible. What did you do this week? How did you feel? If it's too much to journal, simply color in a heart when you do something good for yourself.

how did you FEEL THIS WEEK?

Use the following pages to draw or write about your week. What things happened? Were there any triggering events? How did you handle them? Are you making time to care for yourself and how does that feel? Are you choosing joy? Looking forward to next week, is anything coming up that might be difficult to handle?

week of ______________ to ______________

remember your BREATHWORK

Set a timer for 2 minutes each day just to breathe deeply. Breathe in deeply through your nose for a count of 4-6 and then slowly release that breath. If you can't do two full minutes, start by trying to breathe deeply in and out at least 3 times until you can increase the time. Conscious breathwork reduces the effects of PTSD and stress from trauma. It promotes calmness and well-being.

Check off or color in the heart for each day you successfully did your breathwork and then write how you felt after your breathwork session.

M ♡ ______________________________

T ♡ ______________________________

W ♡ ______________________________

T ♡ ______________________________

F ♡ ______________________________

S ♡ ______________________________

S ♡ ______________________________

practice your GRATITUDE

Finish this sentence each day: TODAY I AM GRATEFUL FOR...
If you're struggling to find gratitude, choose from the Affirmation Bank in the front of the planner and write it in each day.

M ♡ ______________________________

T ♡ ______________________________

W ♡ ______________________________

T ♡ ______________________________

F ♡ ______________________________

S ♡ ______________________________

S ♡ ______________________________

practice your SELF-CARE

Color in a heart for each self-care activity you did this week.

♡

♡

♡

♡

♡

MAKING TIME FOR SELF-CARE

Try to fit in small moments of self-care when possible. What did you do this week? How did you feel? If it's too much to journal, simply color in a heart when you do something good for yourself.

how did you FEEL THIS WEEK?

Use the following pages to draw or write about your week. What things happened? Were there any triggering events? How did you handle them? Are you making time to care for yourself and how does that feel? Are you choosing joy? Looking forward to next week, is anything coming up that might be difficult to handle?

week of __________ to __________

Set a timer for 2 minutes each day just to breathe deeply. Breathe in deeply through your nose for a count of 4-6 and then slowly release that breath. If you can't do two full minutes, start by trying to breathe deeply in and out at least 3 times until you can increase the time. Conscious breathwork reduces the effects of PTSD and stress from trauma. It promotes calmness and well-being.

Check off or color in the heart for each day you successfully did your breathwork and then write how you felt after your breathwork session.

M ♡ ____________________

T ♡ ____________________

W ♡ ____________________

T ♡ ____________________

F ♡ ____________________

S ♡ ____________________

S ♡ ____________________

practice your GRATITUDE

Finish this sentence each day: TODAY I AM GRATEFUL FOR...
If you're struggling to find gratitude, choose from the Affirmation Bank in the front of the planner and write it in each day.

M ♡ ______

T ♡ ______

W ♡ ______

T ♡ ______

F ♡ ______

S ♡ ______

S ♡ ______

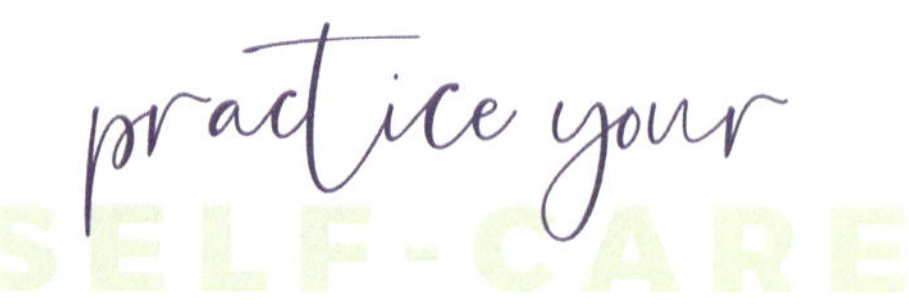

Color in a heart for each self-care activity you did this week.

MAKING TIME FOR SELF-CARE

Try to fit in small moments of self-care when possible. What did you do this week? How did you feel? If it's too much to journal, simply color in a heart when you do something good for yourself.

how did you FEEL THIS WEEK?

Use the following pages to draw or write about your week. What things happened? Were there any triggering events? How did you handle them? Are you making time to care for yourself and how does that feel? Are you choosing joy? Looking forward to next week, is anything coming up that might be difficult to handle?

week of ____________ to ____________

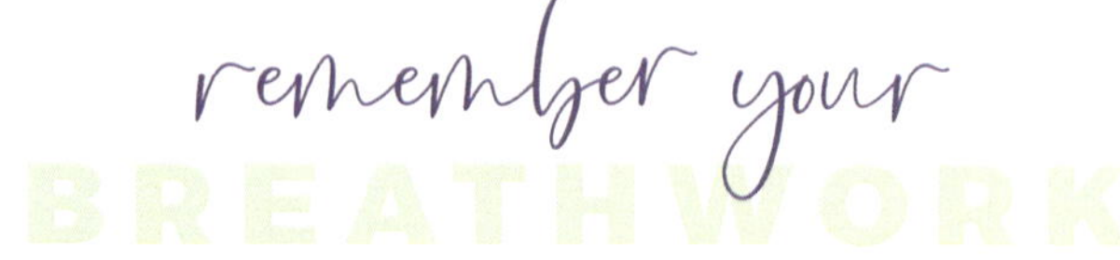

Set a timer for 2 minutes each day just to breathe deeply. Breathe in deeply through your nose for a count of 4-6 and then slowly release that breath. If you can't do two full minutes, start by trying to breathe deeply in and out at least 3 times until you can increase the time. Conscious breath-work reduces the effects of PTSD and stress from trauma. It promotes calmness and well-being.

Check off or color in the heart for each day you successfully did your breathwork and then write how you felt after your breath-work session.

M ♡ ________________________________

T ♡ ________________________________

W ♡ ________________________________

T ♡ ________________________________

F ♡ ________________________________

S ♡ ________________________________

S ♡ ________________________________

practice your GRATITUDE

Finish this sentence each day: TODAY I AM GRATEFUL FOR...

If you're struggling to find gratitude, choose from the Affirmation Bank in the front of the planner and write it in each day.

M ♡ ______________________________

____

____

T ♡ ______________________________

____

____

W ♡ ______________________________

____

____

T ♡ ______________________________

____

____

F ♡ ______________________________

____

____

S ♡ ______________________________

____

____

S ♡ ______________________________

____

____

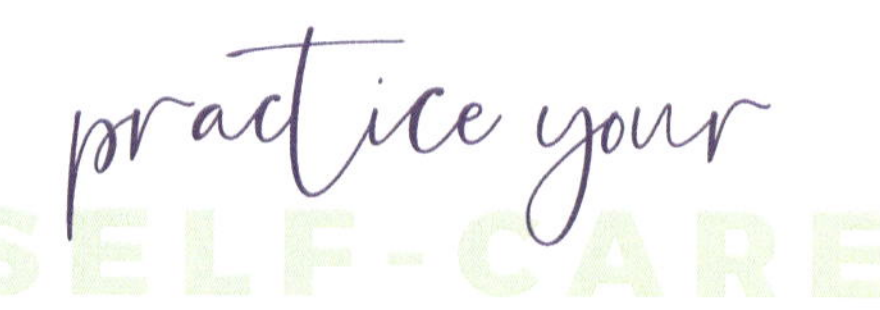

Color in a heart for each self-care activity you did this week.

MAKING TIME FOR SELF-CARE

Try to fit in small moments of self-care when possible. What did you do this week? How did you feel? If it's too much to journal, simply color in a heart when you do something good for yourself.

how did you FEEL THIS WEEK?

Use the following pages to draw or write about your week. What things happened? Were there any triggering events? How did you handle them? Are you making time to care for yourself and how does that feel? Are you choosing joy? Looking forward to next week, is anything coming up that might be difficult to handle?

week of __________ to __________

remember your BREATHWORK

Set a timer for 2 minutes each day just to breathe deeply. Breathe in deeply through your nose for a count of 4-6 and then slowly release that breath. If you can't do two full minutes, start by trying to breathe deeply in and out at least 3 times until you can increase the time. Conscious breathwork reduces the effects of PTSD and stress from trauma. It promotes calmness and well-being.

Check off or color in the heart for each day you successfully did your breathwork and then write how you felt after your breathwork session.

M ♡ ______________________________

T ♡ ______________________________

W ♡ ______________________________

T ♡ ______________________________

F ♡ ______________________________

S ♡ ______________________________

S ♡ ______________________________

practice your GRATITUDE

Finish this sentence each day: TODAY I AM GRATEFUL FOR...
If you're struggling to find gratitude, choose from the Affirmation Bank in the front of the planner and write it in each day.

M ♡ ______________________________

____

____

T ♡ ______________________________

____

____

W ♡ ______________________________

____

____

T ♡ ______________________________

____

____

F ♡ ______________________________

____

____

S ♡ ______________________________

____

____

S ♡ ______________________________

____

____

Color in a heart for each self-care activity you did this week.

MAKING TIME FOR SELF-CARE

Try to fit in small moments of self-care when possible. What did you do this week? How did you feel? If it's too much to journal, simply color in a heart when you do something good for yourself.

how did you FEEL THIS WEEK?

Use the following pages to draw or write about your week. What things happened? Were there any triggering events? How did you handle them? Are you making time to care for yourself and how does that feel? Are you choosing joy? Looking forward to next week, is anything coming up that might be difficult to handle?

REFLECTION

You've made it a month! Are you noticing any changes in how you feel? How are your emotions? Did you experience any aha moments? Are you making time for yourself? What about the important people in your life? Use these pages to write or draw your observations about the past month.

monthly CHECK-IN

SELF-CARE

Fill in a heart for each week you did at least 2 self-care activities.

♡ ♡ ♡ ♡ ♡

WHICH SELF-CARE ACTIVITIES DID YOU DO AND HOW DID YOU FEEL AFTER COMPLETING THEM?

THINGS TO TRY

List what you want to add to your self-care next month. Refer to the self-care ideas bank if you need inspiration.

monthly CHECK-IN

REACHING OUT

It's easy to get lost in our own pain and shut out the other important members of our lives. Remember: the people who are the happiest have strong relationships with others. While it may be difficult to reach out in a time that you feel people should be checking in on you, try not to isolate yourself.

Who are the important people in your life? Who will you make an effort to reach out to? If you have other children, how are they doing? How is your spouse? Who is someone you were close to before that you haven't heard from in a while?

List three people you commit to reaching out to via text, phone call, email, snail mail, or getting together with. Think about birthdays, anniversaries, and other special events and list those out. Be sure to add to your calendar.

I WILL REACH OUT TO...

♡ ______________________________

♡ ______________________________

♡ ______________________________

UPCOMING EVENTS INCLUDE...

____

____

____

____

____

____

IT'S OKAY TO

let go of pain

WHILE KEEPING
THE LOVE INTACT.

QUARTERLY CHECKIN

quarterly CHECK-IN

RELATIONSHIPS

How is your spouse and/or children doing? Are you making time to find ways to bond and grow together? Use the space below to write about your family.

OTHER RELATIONSHIPS

Who are the most significant people in your life outside of your family? What efforts have you made to spend time with them?

LOOK AHEAD

What's coming up? What events or dates might be triggering? How can you mitigate the impact of these by planning time or events with people you care about?

REMEMBERING MY CHILD

Reflect on the last few months. You can write a letter to your child, or write about any new friendships, wins, or challenges within your community. How have things changed in the past three months? What is working on your path for healing? What is not working?

I GIVE MYSELF

permission

TO LIVE FULLY,
EVEN WHILE
I GRIEVE.

month 4

SUN	MON	TUE	WED	THU	FRI	SAT

week of ____________ to ____________

Set a timer for 2 minutes each day just to breathe deeply. Breathe in deeply through your nose for a count of 4-6 and then slowly release that breath. If you can't do two full minutes, start by trying to breathe deeply in and out at least 3 times until you can increase the time. Conscious breath-work reduces the effects of PTSD and stress from trauma. It promotes calmness and well-being.

Check off or color in the heart for each day you successfully did your breathwork and then write how you felt after your breath-work session.

M ♡ ______________________________

T ♡ ______________________________

W ♡ ______________________________

T ♡ ______________________________

F ♡ ______________________________

S ♡ ______________________________

S ♡ ______________________________

practice your GRATITUDE

Finish this sentence each day: TODAY I AM GRATEFUL FOR...
If you're struggling to find gratitude, choose from the Affirmation Bank in the front of the planner and write it in each day.

M ♡ ______

T ♡ ______

W ♡ ______

T ♡ ______

F ♡ ______

S ♡ ______

S ♡ ______

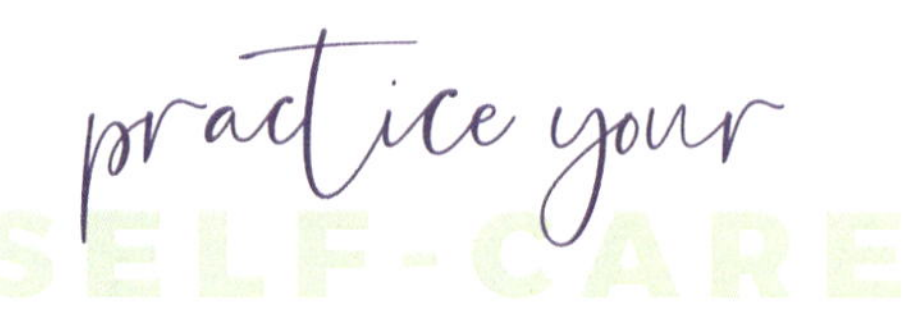

practice your SELF-CARE

Color in a heart for each self-care activity you did this week.

MAKING TIME FOR SELF-CARE

Try to fit in small moments of self-care when possible. What did you do this week? How did you feel? If it's too much to journal, simply color in a heart when you do something good for yourself.

how did you FEEL THIS WEEK?

Use the following pages to draw or write about your week. What things happened? Were there any triggering events? How did you handle them? Are you making time to care for yourself and how does that feel? Are you choosing joy? Looking forward to next week, is anything coming up that might be difficult to handle?

week of ______________ to ______________

remember your BREATHWORK

Set a timer for 2 minutes each day just to breathe deeply. Breathe in deeply through your nose for a count of 4-6 and then slowly release that breath. If you can't do two full minutes, start by trying to breathe deeply in and out at least 3 times until you can increase the time. Conscious breathwork reduces the effects of PTSD and stress from trauma. It promotes calmness and well-being.

Check off or color in the heart for each day you successfully did your breathwork and then write how you felt after your breathwork session.

M ♡ ____

T ♡ ____

W ♡ ____

T ♡ ____

F ♡ ____

S ♡ ____

S ♡ ____

practice your GRATITUDE

Finish this sentence each day: TODAY I AM GRATEFUL FOR...
If you're struggling to find gratitude, choose from the Affirmation Bank in the front of the planner and write it in each day.

M ♡

T ♡

W ♡

T ♡

F ♡

S ♡

S ♡

practice your SELF-CARE

Color in a heart for each self-care activity you did this week.

♡

____

____

♡

____

____

♡

____

____

♡

____

____

♡

____

____

MAKING TIME FOR SELF-CARE

Try to fit in small moments of self-care when possible. What did you do this week? How did you feel? If it's too much to journal, simply color in a heart when you do something good for yourself.

how did you FEEL THIS WEEK?

Use the following pages to draw or write about your week. What things happened? Were there any triggering events? How did you handle them? Are you making time to care for yourself and how does that feel? Are you choosing joy? Looking forward to next week, is anything coming up that might be difficult to handle?

week of ____________ to ____________

remember your BREATHWORK

Set a timer for 2 minutes each day just to breathe deeply. Breathe in deeply through your nose for a count of 4-6 and then slowly release that breath. If you can't do two full minutes, start by trying to breathe deeply in and out at least 3 times until you can increase the time. Conscious breathwork reduces the effects of PTSD and stress from trauma. It promotes calmness and well-being.

Check off or color in the heart for each day you successfully did your breathwork and then write how you felt after your breathwork session.

M ♡ ____________________

T ♡ ____________________

W ♡ ____________________

T ♡ ____________________

F ♡ ____________________

S ♡ ____________________

S ♡ ____________________

practice your GRATITUDE

Finish this sentence each day: TODAY I AM GRATEFUL FOR...
If you're struggling to find gratitude, choose from the Affirmation Bank in the front of the planner and write it in each day.

M ♡ ____________________

T ♡ ____________________

W ♡ ____________________

T ♡ ____________________

F ♡ ____________________

S ♡ ____________________

S ♡ ____________________

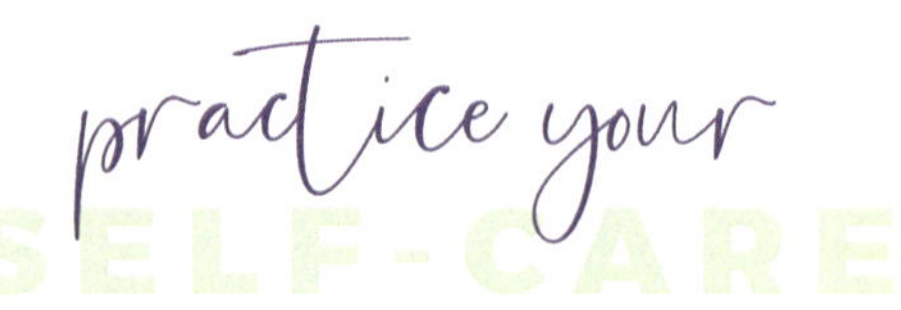

Color in a heart for each self-care activity you did this week.

♡

♡

♡

♡

♡

MAKING TIME FOR SELF-CARE

Try to fit in small moments of self-care when possible. What did you do this week? How did you feel? If it's too much to journal, simply color in a heart when you do something good for yourself.

how did you FEEL THIS WEEK?

Use the following pages to draw or write about your week. What things happened? Were there any triggering events? How did you handle them? Are you making time to care for yourself and how does that feel? Are you choosing joy? Looking forward to next week, is anything coming up that might be difficult to handle?

week of ____________ to ____________

remember your BREATHWORK

Set a timer for 2 minutes each day just to breathe deeply. Breathe in deeply through your nose for a count of 4-6 and then slowly release that breath. If you can't do two full minutes, start by trying to breathe deeply in and out at least 3 times until you can increase the time. Conscious breath-work reduces the effects of PTSD and stress from trauma. It promotes calmness and well-being.

Check off or color in the heart for each day you successfully did your breathwork and then write how you felt after your breath-work session.

M ♡ ____

T ♡ ____

W ♡ ____

T ♡ ____

F ♡ ____

S ♡ ____

S ♡ ____

practice your GRATITUDE

Finish this sentence each day: TODAY I AM GRATEFUL FOR...
If you're struggling to find gratitude, choose from the Affirmation Bank in the front of the planner and write it in each day.

M ♡ ______________________________

T ♡ ______________________________

W ♡ ______________________________

T ♡ ______________________________

F ♡ ______________________________

S ♡ ______________________________

S ♡ ______________________________

practice your SELF-CARE

Color in a heart for each self-care activity you did this week.

MAKING TIME FOR SELF-CARE

Try to fit in small moments of self-care when possible. What did you do this week? How did you feel? If it's too much to journal, simply color in a heart when you do something good for yourself.

how did you FEEL THIS WEEK?

Use the following pages to draw or write about your week. What things happened? Were there any triggering events? How did you handle them? Are you making time to care for yourself and how does that feel? Are you choosing joy? Looking forward to next week, is anything coming up that might be difficult to handle?

week of ____________ to ____________

remember your BREATHWORK

Set a timer for 2 minutes each day just to breathe deeply. Breathe in deeply through your nose for a count of 4-6 and then slowly release that breath. If you can't do two full minutes, start by trying to breathe deeply in and out at least 3 times until you can increase the time. Conscious breath-work reduces the effects of PTSD and stress from trauma. It promotes calmness and well-being.

Check off or color in the heart for each day you successfully did your breathwork and then write how you felt after your breath-work session.

M ♡ ______________________________

T ♡ ______________________________

W ♡ ______________________________

T ♡ ______________________________

F ♡ ______________________________

S ♡ ______________________________

S ♡ ______________________________

practice your GRATITUDE

Finish this sentence each day: TODAY I AM GRATEFUL FOR...
If you're struggling to find gratitude, choose from the Affirmation Bank in the front of the planner and write it in each day.

M ♡ ______________________________

T ♡ ______________________________

W ♡ ______________________________

T ♡ ______________________________

F ♡ ______________________________

S ♡ ______________________________

S ♡ ______________________________

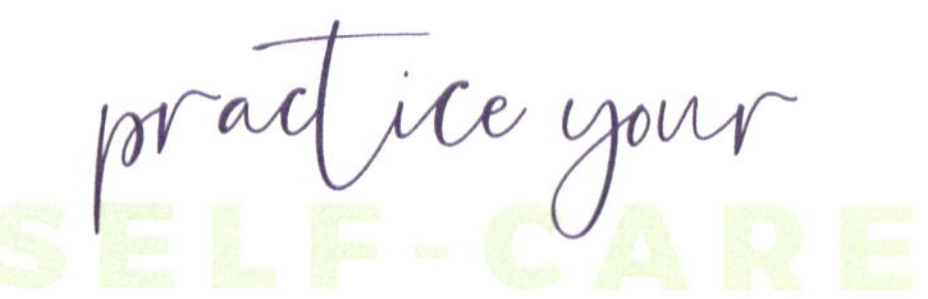

Color in a heart for each self-care activity you did this week.

MAKING TIME FOR SELF-CARE

Try to fit in small moments of self-care when possible. What did you do this week? How did you feel? If it's too much to journal, simply color in a heart when you do something good for yourself.

how did you FEEL THIS WEEK?

Use the following pages to draw or write about your week. What things happened? Were there any triggering events? How did you handle them? Are you making time to care for yourself and how does that feel? Are you choosing joy? Looking forward to next week, is anything coming up that might be difficult to handle?

REFLECTION

You've made it a month! Are you noticing any changes in how you feel? How are your emotions? Did you experience any aha moments? Are you making time for yourself? What about the important people in your life? Use these pages to write or draw your observations about the past month.

monthly CHECK-IN

SELF-CARE

Fill in a heart for each week you did at least 2 self-care activities.

♡ ♡ ♡ ♡ ♡

WHICH SELF-CARE ACTIVITIES DID YOU DO AND HOW DID YOU FEEL AFTER COMPLETING THEM?

THINGS TO TRY

List what you want to add to your self-care next month. Refer to the self-care ideas bank if you need inspiration.

monthly CHECK-IN

REACHING OUT

It's easy to get lost in our own pain and shut out the other important members of our lives. Remember: the people who are the happiest have strong relationships with others. While it may be difficult to reach out in a time that you feel people should be checking in on you, try not to isolate yourself.

Who are the important people in your life? Who will you make an effort to reach out to? If you have other children, how are they doing? How is your spouse? Who is someone you were close to before that you haven't heard from in a while?

List three people you commit to reaching out to via text, phone call, email, snail mail, or getting together with. Think about birthdays, anniversaries, and other special events and list those out. Be sure to add to your calendar.

I WILL REACH OUT TO...

♡ ____________________

♡ ____________________

♡ ____________________

UPCOMING EVENTS INCLUDE...

____

____

____

____

____

____

EACH DAY I HEAL
A LITTLE MORE,

and it's okay

TO ACKNOWLEDGE
THAT PROGRESS.

month 5

SUN	MON	TUE	WED	THU	FRI	SAT

week of ____________ to ____________

Set a timer for 2 minutes each day just to breathe deeply. Breathe in deeply through your nose for a count of 4-6 and then slowly release that breath. If you can't do two full minutes, start by trying to breathe deeply in and out at least 3 times until you can increase the time. Conscious breathwork reduces the effects of PTSD and stress from trauma. It promotes calmness and well-being.

Check off or color in the heart for each day you successfully did your breathwork and then write how you felt after your breathwork session.

M ♡ ____

T ♡ ____

W ♡ ____

T ♡ ____

F ♡ ____

S ♡ ____

S ♡ ____

practice your GRATITUDE

Finish this sentence each day: TODAY I AM GRATEFUL FOR...
If you're struggling to find gratitude, choose from the Affirmation Bank in the front of the planner and write it in each day.

M

T

W

T

F

S

S

practice your SELF-CARE

Color in a heart for each self-care activity you did this week.

MAKING TIME FOR SELF-CARE

Try to fit in small moments of self-care when possible. What did you do this week? How did you feel? If it's too much to journal, simply color in a heart when you do something good for yourself.

how did you FEEL THIS WEEK?

Use the following pages to draw or write about your week. What things happened? Were there any triggering events? How did you handle them? Are you making time to care for yourself and how does that feel? Are you choosing joy? Looking forward to next week, is anything coming up that might be difficult to handle?

week of ____________ to ____________

remember your BREATHWORK

Set a timer for 2 minutes each day just to breathe deeply. Breathe in deeply through your nose for a count of 4-6 and then slowly release that breath. If you can't do two full minutes, start by trying to breathe deeply in and out at least 3 times until you can increase the time. Conscious breathwork reduces the effects of PTSD and stress from trauma. It promotes calmness and well-being.

Check off or color in the heart for each day you successfully did your breathwork and then write how you felt after your breathwork session.

M ♡ ____________________

T ♡ ____________________

W ♡ ____________________

T ♡ ____________________

F ♡ ____________________

S ♡ ____________________

S ♡ ____________________

practice your GRATITUDE

Finish this sentence each day: TODAY I AM GRATEFUL FOR...
If you're struggling to find gratitude, choose from the Affirmation Bank in the front of the planner and write it in each day.

M ♡ ______________________________

____

____

T ♡ ______________________________

____

____

W ♡ ______________________________

____

____

T ♡ ______________________________

____

____

F ♡ ______________________________

____

____

S ♡ ______________________________

____

____

S ♡ ______________________________

____

____

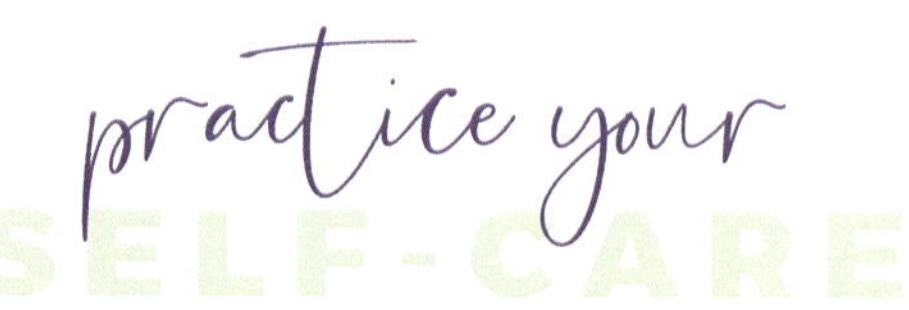

Color in a heart for each self-care activity you did this week.

MAKING TIME FOR SELF-CARE

Try to fit in small moments of self-care when possible. What did you do this week? How did you feel? If it's too much to journal, simply color in a heart when you do something good for yourself.

how did you FEEL THIS WEEK?

Use the following pages to draw or write about your week. What things happened? Were there any triggering events? How did you handle them? Are you making time to care for yourself and how does that feel? Are you choosing joy? Looking forward to next week, is anything coming up that might be difficult to handle?

week of ________ to ________

remember your BREATHWORK

Set a timer for 2 minutes each day just to breathe deeply. Breathe in deeply through your nose for a count of 4-6 and then slowly release that breath. If you can't do two full minutes, start by trying to breathe deeply in and out at least 3 times until you can increase the time. Conscious breath-work reduces the effects of PTSD and stress from trauma. It promotes calmness and well-being.

Check off or color in the heart for each day you successfully did your breathwork and then write how you felt after your breath-work session.

M ♡ ____________________

T ♡ ____________________

W ♡ ____________________

T ♡ ____________________

F ♡ ____________________

S ♡ ____________________

S ♡ ____________________

practice your GRATITUDE

Finish this sentence each day: TODAY I AM GRATEFUL FOR...
If you're struggling to find gratitude, choose from the Affirmation Bank in the front of the planner and write it in each day.

M ♡ ______

T ♡ ______

W ♡ ______

T ♡ ______

F ♡ ______

S ♡ ______

S ♡ ______

practice your SELF-CARE

Color in a heart for each self-care activity you did this week.

MAKING TIME FOR SELF-CARE

Try to fit in small moments of self-care when possible. What did you do this week? How did you feel? If it's too much to journal, simply color in a heart when you do something good for yourself.

how did you FEEL THIS WEEK?

Use the following pages to draw or write about your week. What things happened? Were there any triggering events? How did you handle them? Are you making time to care for yourself and how does that feel? Are you choosing joy? Looking forward to next week, is anything coming up that might be difficult to handle?

week of ____________ to ____________

Set a timer for 2 minutes each day just to breathe deeply. Breathe in deeply through your nose for a count of 4-6 and then slowly release that breath. If you can't do two full minutes, start by trying to breathe deeply in and out at least 3 times until you can increase the time. Conscious breathwork reduces the effects of PTSD and stress from trauma. It promotes calmness and well-being.

Check off or color in the heart for each day you successfully did your breathwork and then write how you felt after your breathwork session.

M ♡ ____________________

T ♡ ____________________

W ♡ ____________________

T ♡ ____________________

F ♡ ____________________

S ♡ ____________________

S ♡ ____________________

practice your GRATITUDE

Finish this sentence each day: TODAY I AM GRATEFUL FOR...
If you're struggling to find gratitude, choose from the Affirmation Bank in the front of the planner and write it in each day.

M ♡ ______________________________

T ♡ ______________________________

W ♡ ______________________________

T ♡ ______________________________

F ♡ ______________________________

S ♡ ______________________________

S ♡ ______________________________

Color in a heart for each self-care activity you did this week.

MAKING TIME FOR SELF-CARE

Try to fit in small moments of self-care when possible. What did you do this week? How did you feel? If it's too much to journal, simply color in a heart when you do something good for yourself.

how did you FEEL THIS WEEK?

Use the following pages to draw or write about your week. What things happened? Were there any triggering events? How did you handle them? Are you making time to care for yourself and how does that feel? Are you choosing joy? Looking forward to next week, is anything coming up that might be difficult to handle?

week of ______________ to ______________

Set a timer for 2 minutes each day just to breathe deeply. Breathe in deeply through your nose for a count of 4-6 and then slowly release that breath. If you can't do two full minutes, start by trying to breathe deeply in and out at least 3 times until you can increase the time. Conscious breathwork reduces the effects of PTSD and stress from trauma. It promotes calmness and well-being.

Check off or color in the heart for each day you successfully did your breathwork and then write how you felt after your breathwork session.

M ♡ ______________________________

T ♡ ______________________________

W ♡ ______________________________

T ♡ ______________________________

F ♡ ______________________________

S ♡ ______________________________

S ♡ ______________________________

practice your GRATITUDE

Finish this sentence each day: TODAY I AM GRATEFUL FOR...
If you're struggling to find gratitude, choose from the Affirmation Bank in the front of the planner and write it in each day.

M ♡ ______________________________

T ♡ ______________________________

W ♡ ______________________________

T ♡ ______________________________

F ♡ ______________________________

S ♡ ______________________________

S ♡ ______________________________

Color in a heart for each self-care activity you did this week.

MAKING TIME FOR SELF-CARE

Try to fit in small moments of self-care when possible. What did you do this week? How did you feel? If it's too much to journal, simply color in a heart when you do something good for yourself.

how did you FEEL THIS WEEK?

Use the following pages to draw or write about your week. What things happened? Were there any triggering events? How did you handle them? Are you making time to care for yourself and how does that feel? Are you choosing joy? Looking forward to next week, is anything coming up that might be difficult to handle?

monthly CHECK-IN

REFLECTION

You've made it a month! Are you noticing any changes in how you feel? How are your emotions? Did you experience any aha moments? Are you making time for yourself? What about the important people in your life? Use these pages to write or draw your observations about the past month.

monthly CHECK-IN

SELF-CARE

Fill in a heart for each week you did at least 2 self-care activities.

♡ ♡ ♡ ♡ ♡

WHICH SELF-CARE ACTIVITIES DID YOU DO AND HOW DID YOU FEEL AFTER COMPLETING THEM?

THINGS TO TRY

List what you want to add to your self-care next month. Refer to the self-care ideas bank if you need inspiration.

monthly CHECK-IN

REACHING OUT

It's easy to get lost in our own pain and shut out the other important members of our lives. Remember: the people who are the happiest have strong relationships with others. While it may be difficult to reach out in a time that you feel people should be checking in on you, try not to isolate yourself.

Who are the important people in your life? Who will you make an effort to reach out to? If you have other children, how are they doing? How is your spouse? Who is someone you were close to before that you haven't heard from in a while?

List three people you commit to reaching out to via text, phone call, email, snail mail, or getting together with. Think about birthdays, anniversaries, and other special events and list those out. Be sure to add to your calendar.

I WILL REACH OUT TO...

♡ ____

♡ ____

♡ ____

UPCOMING EVENTS INCLUDE...

____

____

____

____

____

____

I AM WORTHY OF

happiness and love,

NOW AND ALWAYS.

month 6 ____________________

SUN	MON	TUE	WED	THU	FRI	SAT

week of __________ to __________

remember your BREATHWORK

Set a timer for 2 minutes each day just to breathe deeply. Breathe in deeply through your nose for a count of 4-6 and then slowly release that breath. If you can't do two full minutes, start by trying to breathe deeply in and out at least 3 times until you can increase the time. Conscious breath-work reduces the effects of PTSD and stress from trauma. It promotes calmness and well-being.

Check off or color in the heart for each day you successfully did your breathwork and then write how you felt after your breath-work session.

M ♡ ____________________

T ♡ ____________________

W ♡ ____________________

T ♡ ____________________

F ♡ ____________________

S ♡ ____________________

S ♡ ____________________

practice your GRATITUDE

Finish this sentence each day: TODAY I AM GRATEFUL FOR...
If you're struggling to find gratitude, choose from the Affirmation Bank in the front of the planner and write it in each day.

M ♡ ______________________________

T ♡ ______________________________

W ♡ ______________________________

T ♡ ______________________________

F ♡ ______________________________

S ♡ ______________________________

S ♡ ______________________________

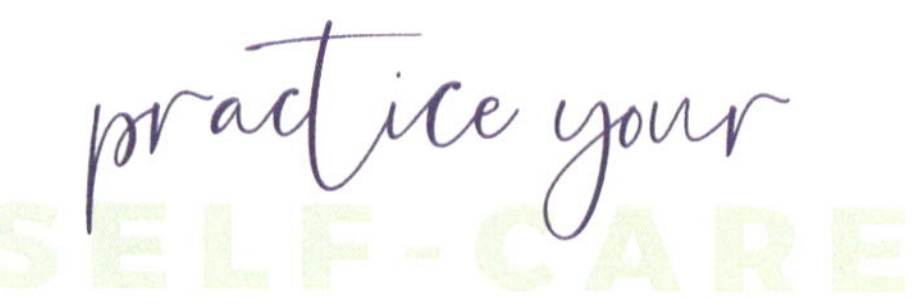

Color in a heart for each self-care activity you did this week.

MAKING TIME FOR SELF-CARE

Try to fit in small moments of self-care when possible. What did you do this week? How did you feel? If it's too much to journal, simply color in a heart when you do something good for yourself.

how did you FEEL THIS WEEK?

Use the following pages to draw or write about your week. What things happened? Were there any triggering events? How did you handle them? Are you making time to care for yourself and how does that feel? Are you choosing joy? Looking forward to next week, is anything coming up that might be difficult to handle?

week of __________ to __________

remember your BREATHWORK

Set a timer for 2 minutes each day just to breathe deeply. Breathe in deeply through your nose for a count of 4-6 and then slowly release that breath. If you can't do two full minutes, start by trying to breathe deeply in and out at least 3 times until you can increase the time. Conscious breathwork reduces the effects of PTSD and stress from trauma. It promotes calmness and well-being.

Check off or color in the heart for each day you successfully did your breathwork and then write how you felt after your breathwork session.

M ♡ ______________________________

T ♡ ______________________________

W ♡ ______________________________

T ♡ ______________________________

F ♡ ______________________________

S ♡ ______________________________

S ♡ ______________________________

practice your GRATITUDE

Finish this sentence each day: TODAY I AM GRATEFUL FOR...
If you're struggling to find gratitude, choose from the Affirmation Bank in the front of the planner and write it in each day.

M ♡ ______

T ♡ ______

W ♡ ______

T ♡ ______

F ♡ ______

S ♡ ______

S ♡ ______

Color in a heart for each self-care activity you did this week.

♡

♡

♡

♡

♡

MAKING TIME FOR SELF-CARE

Try to fit in small moments of self-care when possible. What did you do this week? How did you feel? If it's too much to journal, simply color in a heart when you do something good for yourself.

how did you FEEL THIS WEEK?

Use the following pages to draw or write about your week. What things happened? Were there any triggering events? How did you handle them? Are you making time to care for yourself and how does that feel? Are you choosing joy? Looking forward to next week, is anything coming up that might be difficult to handle?

week of ______________ to ______________

Set a timer for 2 minutes each day just to breathe deeply. Breathe in deeply through your nose for a count of 4-6 and then slowly release that breath. If you can't do two full minutes, start by trying to breathe deeply in and out at least 3 times until you can increase the time. Conscious breath-work reduces the effects of PTSD and stress from trauma. It promotes calmness and well-being.

Check off or color in the heart for each day you successfully did your breathwork and then write how you felt after your breath-work session.

M ♡ ____________________

T ♡ ____________________

W ♡ ____________________

T ♡ ____________________

F ♡ ____________________

S ♡ ____________________

S ♡ ____________________

practice your GRATITUDE

Finish this sentence each day: TODAY I AM GRATEFUL FOR...
If you're struggling to find gratitude, choose from the Affirmation Bank in the front of the planner and write it in each day.

M ♡ ______________________________

T ♡ ______________________________

W ♡ ______________________________

T ♡ ______________________________

F ♡ ______________________________

S ♡ ______________________________

S ♡ ______________________________

practice your SELF-CARE

Color in a heart for each self-care activity you did this week.

♡

♡

♡

♡

♡

MAKING TIME FOR SELF-CARE

Try to fit in small moments of self-care when possible. What did you do this week? How did you feel? If it's too much to journal, simply color in a heart when you do something good for yourself.

how did you FEEL THIS WEEK?

Use the following pages to draw or write about your week. What things happened? Were there any triggering events? How did you handle them? Are you making time to care for yourself and how does that feel? Are you choosing joy? Looking forward to next week, is anything coming up that might be difficult to handle?

week of ____________ to ____________

remember your BREATHWORK

Set a timer for 2 minutes each day just to breathe deeply. Breathe in deeply through your nose for a count of 4-6 and then slowly release that breath. If you can't do two full minutes, start by trying to breathe deeply in and out at least 3 times until you can increase the time. Conscious breathwork reduces the effects of PTSD and stress from trauma. It promotes calmness and well-being.

Check off or color in the heart for each day you successfully did your breathwork and then write how you felt after your breathwork session.

M ♡ ____

T ♡ ____

W ♡ ____

T ♡ ____

F ♡ ____

S ♡ ____

S ♡ ____

practice your GRATITUDE

Finish this sentence each day: TODAY I AM GRATEFUL FOR...
If you're struggling to find gratitude, choose from the Affirmation Bank in the front of the planner and write it in each day.

M ♡ ______

T ♡ ______

W ♡ ______

T ♡ ______

F ♡ ______

S ♡ ______

S ♡ ______

Color in a heart for each self-care activity you did this week.

MAKING TIME FOR SELF-CARE

Try to fit in small moments of self-care when possible. What did you do this week? How did you feel? If it's too much to journal, simply color in a heart when you do something good for yourself.

how did you FEEL THIS WEEK?

Use the following pages to draw or write about your week. What things happened? Were there any triggering events? How did you handle them? Are you making time to care for yourself and how does that feel? Are you choosing joy? Looking forward to next week, is anything coming up that might be difficult to handle?

week of ______________ to ______________

remember your BREATHWORK

Set a timer for 2 minutes each day just to breathe deeply. Breathe in deeply through your nose for a count of 4-6 and then slowly release that breath. If you can't do two full minutes, start by trying to breathe deeply in and out at least 3 times until you can increase the time. Conscious breathwork reduces the effects of PTSD and stress from trauma. It promotes calmness and well-being.

Check off or color in the heart for each day you successfully did your breathwork and then write how you felt after your breathwork session.

M ♡ ______________________________

T ♡ ______________________________

W ♡ ______________________________

T ♡ ______________________________

F ♡ ______________________________

S ♡ ______________________________

S ♡ ______________________________

practice your GRATITUDE

Finish this sentence each day: TODAY I AM GRATEFUL FOR...
If you're struggling to find gratitude, choose from the Affirmation Bank in the front of the planner and write it in each day.

M ♡ __________

T ♡ __________

W ♡ __________

T ♡ __________

F ♡ __________

S ♡ __________

S ♡ __________

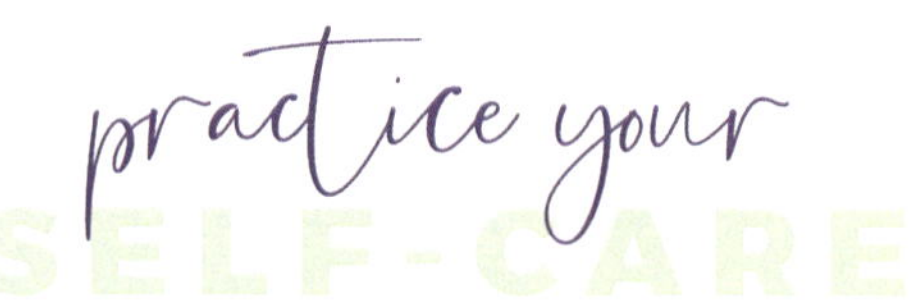

Color in a heart for each self-care activity you did this week.

♡

♡

♡

♡

♡

MAKING TIME FOR SELF-CARE

Try to fit in small moments of self-care when possible. What did you do this week? How did you feel? If it's too much to journal, simply color in a heart when you do something good for yourself.

how did you FEEL THIS WEEK?

Use the following pages to draw or write about your week. What things happened? Were there any triggering events? How did you handle them? Are you making time to care for yourself and how does that feel? Are you choosing joy? Looking forward to next week, is anything coming up that might be difficult to handle?

REFLECTION

You've made it a month! Are you noticing any changes in how you feel? How are your emotions? Did you experience any aha moments? Are you making time for yourself? What about the important people in your life? Use these pages to write or draw your observations about the past month.

monthly CHECK-IN

SELF-CARE

Fill in a heart for each week you did at least 2 self-care activities.

♡ ♡ ♡ ♡ ♡

WHICH SELF-CARE ACTIVITIES DID YOU DO AND HOW DID YOU FEEL AFTER COMPLETING THEM?

THINGS TO TRY

List what you want to add to your self-care next month. Refer to the self-care ideas bank if you need inspiration.

monthly CHECK-IN

REACHING OUT

It's easy to get lost in our own pain and shut out the other important members of our lives. Remember: the people who are the happiest have strong relationships with others. While it may be difficult to reach out in a time that you feel people should be checking in on you, try not to isolate yourself.

Who are the important people in your life? Who will you make an effort to reach out to? If you have other children, how are they doing? How is your spouse? Who is someone you were close to before that you haven't heard from in a while?

List three people you commit to reaching out to via text, phone call, email, snail mail, or getting together with. Think about birthdays, anniversaries, and other special events and list those out. Be sure to add to your calendar.

I WILL REACH OUT TO...

♡ ______________________________

♡ ______________________________

♡ ______________________________

UPCOMING EVENTS INCLUDE...

____

____

____

____

____

____

MY CAPACITY
FOR JOY IS
expanding,
EVEN AS I
REMEMBER YOU.

quarterly CHECK-IN

RELATIONSHIPS

How is your spouse and/or children doing? Are you making time to find ways to bond and grow together? Use the space below to write about your family.

OTHER RELATIONSHIPS

Who are the most significant people in your life outside of your family? What efforts have you made to spend time with them?

LOOK AHEAD

What's coming up? What events or dates might be triggering? How can you mitigate the impact of these by planning time or events with people you care about?

REMEMBERING MY CHILD

Reflect on the last few months. You can write a letter to your child, or write about any new friendships, wins, or challenges within your community. How have things changed in the past three months? What is working on your path for healing? What is not working?